ISAAC ASIMOV'S
Library of the Universe

How Was the Universe Born?

by Isaac Asimov

Gareth Stevens Children's Books
London • Milwaukee

A note from the editors: In the United States and other places — including this book — a billion is the number represented by 1 followed by nine zeroes — 1,000,000,000. In other countries, including Britain, this number is often called 'a thousand million', and one billion would then be represented by 1 followed by 12 zeroes — 1,000,000,000,000: a million million, which is called a 'trillion' in this book.

British Library Cataloguing in Publication Data

Asimov, Isaac, 1920-
    How was the universe born?
    1. Universe — For children
    I. Title   II. Series
    523.1

    ISBN 0-83687-003-4

A Gareth Stevens Children's Books edition

Edited, designed, and produced by
Gareth Stevens Children's Books   31 Newington Green, London N16 9PU

Text copyright © 1989 by Nightfall, Inc.
End matter copyright © 1989 by Gareth Stevens, Inc. and Martin Greenberg
Format copyright © 1989 by Gareth Stevens, Inc.

First published in the United States and Canada by Gareth Stevens, Inc.
First published in the United Kingdom in 1989 by Gareth Stevens Children's Books

Cover painting © Julian Baum
Designer: Laurie Shock
Picture research: Kathy Keller
Artwork commissioning: Kathy Keller and Laurie Shock
Project editors: Mark Sachner and Scott Enk
Technical advisers and consulting editors: Greg Walz-Chojnacki and Francis Reddy

1 2 3 4 5 6 7 8 9 9 94 93 92 91 90 89

CONTENTS

Nowadays, we have seen close-up views of planets, all the way to distant Uranus. We have mapped Venus through its clouds. We have seen dead volcanoes on Mars and live ones on Io, one of Jupiter's moons. We have put spacecraft with measuring devices on the surfaces of Mars and Venus. Human beings have even walked on our Moon!

But the greatest drama of all is to try to understand the Universe as a whole. We can only begin to try to grasp its vastness and to study all the strange things we find in it. Some of these things — quasars, pulsars, and black holes — we didn't even dream of until the last few decades.

So let's learn a bit about the amazing story of our Universe!

Isaac Asimov

Above: According to ancient Greek myths, the god Helios drove the chariot that carries the Sun across the sky.

Left: Nut, a sky goddess of ancient Egypt.

Right: The stars of summer gleam like jewels on the dome of the night sky.

Primitive Ideas

Long ago, human beings could only suppose that the Universe was what it looked like to them.

The Earth? It seemed to be no more than a round patch of flat ground, not very big. The sky? It seemed to be a solid dome that came down to meet the ground all around, at places not far off. The Sun? It travelled across the sky to give us light and warmth. The sky was blue when the Sun was present, but turned black when it set. In the night sky, there were many, many specks of light — stars — in the dome of the sky. The Moon, which went through a change of shape every month, moved among the stars. A few stars were brighter than the others, and they also moved.

Where Is Earth?

The ancient Greeks said that Earth was a large sphere and thought it was at the centre of the Universe. They thought that the Moon circled around the Earth. Outside the Moon's orbit circled Mercury, Venus, the Sun, Mars, Jupiter, and Saturn. Outside the orbits of all these bodies were the sky and the stars.

In 1543, Copernicus (pronounced co-PER-nic-us) showed that it made more sense to suppose that the Sun was at the centre, and that all the planets moved around it. Earth was one of the planets, and it went around the Sun, too. Beyond that were the stars, but they weren't attached to the sky. Later, Edmund Halley found out that the stars moved, too.

Left: Nicolaus Copernicus — the Polish philosopher, doctor, and astronomer who showed that the planets circle the Sun.

Lower left: the Copernican system. The Sun lies in the centre and Earth circles around it.

Below: Star trails in a time-exposure photo of the night sky. From where we stand on Earth, the Sun, Moon, planets, and stars all seem to wheel across the sky — small wonder people once thought Earth was the centre of the Universe!

Island Universes

In 1785, William Herschel (HER-shell) showed that all the stars formed a large collection shaped like a lens. We call this collection the Milky Way Galaxy. This is our Galaxy, and it is 100,000 light-years across. Each light-year is about 9.5 trillion km long.

There are other galaxies as well. They look like cloudy patches in the sky, but they are really other galaxies very far away. The closest large galaxy is the Andromeda Galaxy, which is over two million light-years away. Many other galaxies are scattered through space. There might be a hundred billion in all!

The German-born English astronomer William Herschel, discoverer of the planet Uranus. He designed the best telescopes of his time.

If we could view our Milky Way from the outside, it would look like the Great Galaxy in Andromeda, seen here without the aid of a telescope.

Right: Through a telescope, ragged dust clouds appear around the Andromeda Galaxy's core. Over two million light-years away, it's the closest galaxy that resembles our own spiral, the Milky Way. (The white streak across the sky is the light reflected off an artificial satellite moving overhead.)

The Red Shift

In 1842, Christian Doppler explained why anything noisy sounds more shrill when it comes toward you, and sounds deeper when it goes away from you. A similar kind of change, or shift, happens with light.

Austrian scientist Christian Doppler.

Every star sends out light waves. The light appears bluer if the star is coming toward us, and redder if it is moving away. In the 1920s, astronomers found that most galaxies show a 'red shift'. This means that they are moving away from our Galaxy. The farther away they are, the faster they move away from us. The farthest galaxies are moving away at thousands of kilometres a second!

When light from a star or galaxy is spread out into a rainbow of colour, dark lines show up where light has been absorbed by the atoms of that star or galaxy. The lines in the light of distant galaxies are shifted toward ever redder light as we look farther away.

The Outer Limits

The most distant galaxies we can see are hundreds of millions of light-years away. In the 1950s, astronomers discovered certain galaxies that sent out radio waves. These galaxies were studied carefully, and the light waves they sent out looked very strange. In 1963, astronomers found that this was because the light waves were very stretched out.

Galaxies like this are called quasars. Quasars had the largest red shifts known, so they must be very far away. Even the closest quasars are a billion light-years away. One quasar discovered recently is 12 billion light-years away! So when we look at quasars, we are looking back into a time before our Sun was born!

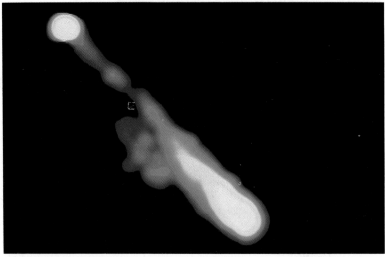

Radio telescopes created this image of a huge gas jet erupting from quasar 3C 273. The jet is a million light-years long!

Right: Appearances can be deceiving. A bridge of gas seems to connect a quasar (top) to a much closer galaxy (below). Astronomers believe that such connections are optical illusions. Colours are added to the picture to bring out faint details.

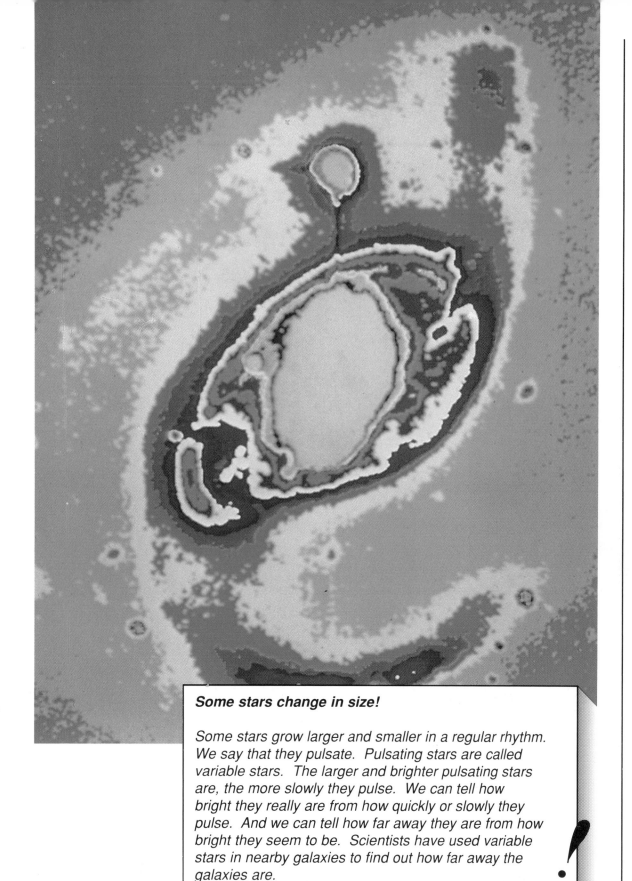

Some stars change in size!

Some stars grow larger and smaller in a regular rhythm. We say that they pulsate. Pulsating stars are called variable stars. The larger and brighter pulsating stars are, the more slowly they pulse. We can tell how bright they really are from how quickly or slowly they pulse. And we can tell how far away they are from how bright they seem to be. Scientists have used variable stars in nearby galaxies to find out how far away the galaxies are.

The Universe — It's a Big Place!

The known planets orbit the Sun in a region about 11 billion km in diameter. That's just a little over a thousandth of a light-year. The nearest star is 4.2 light-years away. That's thousands of times as far away as the farthest planet in our Solar system.

The farthest stars in our Galaxy are 100,000 light-years away. The Andromeda Galaxy is over two million light-years away,

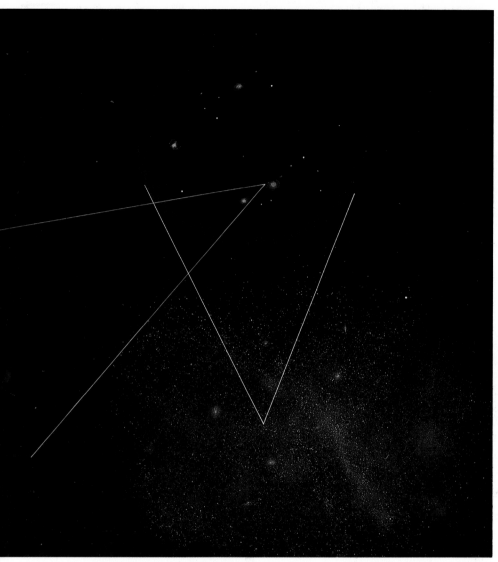

We think of Earth as quite big, but this painting puts us in our place! From left to right, we see that Earth is just one of nine worlds orbiting the Sun. Our Sun itself is just one of 200 billion stars in the Milky Way Galaxy. The Milky Way is but one of many galaxies in our cluster, and one of <u>billions</u> of galaxies in the Universe.

but it's our next-door neighbour. The farthest known quasar is about 12 billion light-years away.

In all the Universe, there are about 100 billion galaxies. And each galaxy contains about 100 billion stars.

Imagine how small our own Earth is in comparison!

A galaxy cluster. The glowing arcs in this picture might be formed by light pulled off course by a tremendous but unidentified source of gravity. No one knows for sure.

The Expanding Universe

Why are all the galaxies moving away from us? Why should the galaxies farthest away from us move away the fastest? What's so special about us?

The answer is that it isn't us at all! Galaxies exist in groups called clusters. Every cluster moves away from every other cluster. No matter what cluster we might live in, the others would be moving away from us. The Universe is always expanding — growing larger. The space between galaxies is getting bigger. But scientists didn't know this until 1929.

Why is the Universe like soap bubbles?

Throughout the Universe, galaxies seem to form lines and even curves. They enclose large spaces in which there seems to be very little matter. If we could look at the Universe from a great distance and see it all at once, we would think it looked like soap bubbles. Galaxies would be like the soap film making up the bubbles. The bubbles themselves would be empty and come in different sizes. Astronomers still don't know why the galaxies were formed in this way.

'Soap bubble' galaxies.

The Big Bang

The Universe is expanding as time goes on. But suppose we look backward in time.

As we go farther and farther back in time, the galaxies move closer and closer together. If we went back in time far enough, all the galaxies would crunch together into a small space.

That was the way it was in the beginning. The whole thing must have exploded in a 'Big Bang'. The Universe is still expanding as a result of that Big Bang. If we measure how fast the Universe is expanding and how long it must have taken to reach its present size, we know that the Big Bang happened 15 to 20 billion years ago.

What came _before_ the Big Bang?

As scientists try to work out the history of the Universe, they reach a point where the laws of science don't seem to work. They can only describe the Universe a fraction of a second after the Big Bang. But what existed _before_ the birth of the Universe? One scientist thinks the cosmos might have been born from _nothing_. But no one can really say!

Imagine that galaxies are like the raisins in raisin bread dough. The raisins start off fairly close together (top). If you could stand on any one of them as the dough expands (bottom), all the other raisins would appear to be moving away from you. As space expands, all the galaxies appear to be moving away from us.

DERBYSHIRE
SAINT BENEDICT
SCHOOL
COUNTY COUNCIL

19

Whispers of the Big Bang

At the time of the Big Bang, all the matter and energy of the Universe was squeezed into one tiny spot! It must have been very hot — trillions of degrees.

But as the Universe expanded, it cooled off. There are still hot spots, like the stars, but overall, the Universe has become much cooler. The light waves of the vast flash of the Big Bang stretched and grew longer as the Universe cooled. Today, they are very long radio waves.

In 1965, those radio waves were detected. Scientists could hear the last faint whisper of the Big Bang of long ago.

This painting shows the history of our expanding Universe. The bright spot on the left represents the Big Bang itself. As you look further to the right, subatomic particles form, then atoms of matter. Next, gas clumps together to form galaxies. Then, within those galaxies, gas further clumps to make stars and planets.

The Early Universe

Light travels at a speed of 300,000 km a second. If a star is 10 light-years from us, its light takes 10 years to reach us.

Since the Andromeda Galaxy is over two million light-years from us, its light takes over two million years to reach us! This means that the farther out in <u>space</u> we look, the farther back in <u>time</u> we see!

Light from the most distant known quasar takes about 12 billion years to reach us. Since the Big Bang happened about 15 to 20 billion years ago, we see distant quasars as they looked when the Universe was quite young. In 1988, astronomers announced that they had found objects 17 billion light-years away. They were galaxies being formed when the Universe was even younger. We can't see much farther than that!

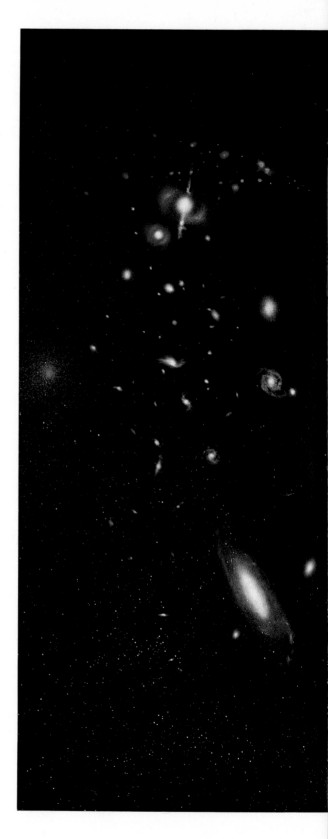

How far is far? The light from our Sun (shown to the upper right of Earth), takes just eight minutes to reach us. Light from the nearest star, Alpha Centauri (the bluish speck shown below Earth), takes 4.2 years. The light we see from the Great Galaxy in Andromeda (the spiral shown lower left) left 2.3 million years ago. And light from the farthest known quasars (upper left) set out 12-15 billion years ago.

How the Universe Changes

Stars stay hot because of nuclear changes in their centres. As a star centre grows hotter, the star expands. Eventually, the star explodes and collapses.

When a very large star explodes, it becomes a supernova. Supernovas spread their material through space. In the Big Bang, only the simplest atoms, hydrogen and helium, were formed, but supernovas spread more complex atoms outward.

Our Sun formed from a cloud with these more complex atoms. Almost all the atoms of Earth — and in ourselves — were formed in stars that exploded as supernovas long ago.

Left: a gas-gulping galaxy? Clouds of gas falling into a bright, young galaxy, II Zwicky 23, have caused a burst of star formation. The new stars are so brilliant that they have caused streaks of light to appear on the telescope's detector.

Left: Special cameras revealed a disk of gas and dust around the star Beta Pictoris. Is this the start of another solar system?

Above: Stars can explode with incredible violence, becoming so bright that they outshine a whole galaxy of normal stars. Supernovas also spread complex elements into space, and the force of the explosions helps stars begin to form.

Left: Galaxy NGC 5128 before (top) and after (bottom) it had a supernova.

A crab in the sky!

In 1054, a supernova only about 5,000 light-years away appeared in the sky. It was brighter than the planet Venus, but a year or so later, it faded away. But what is left of it can still be seen as a small, oddly shaped cloudy patch where the supernova was. It is a cloud of debris left by the explosion. It's called the Crab Nebula because of its shape. The Crab Nebula has been expanding for almost 1,000 years after the explosion. In its centre, there is a tiny neutron star, all that is left of the original giant star that exploded. ●

What Will Happen to the Universe?

When a supernova explodes, what is left of it can collapse into a tiny object with gravity so strong that everything falls in, but nothing comes out. This object is called a black hole. There might be a black hole in the centre of every galaxy.

The Universe may expand forever, or its own gravity might some day slow its expansion, and even stop it. It might then fall back together in a Big Crunch. And maybe a new Universe will form in a new Big Bang.

Maybe there was a Big Crunch, or even many Big Crunches, before the Big Bang that formed our Universe. We don't know if there ever was. We're still trying to understand the Big Bang that created the present Universe. That's a big enough puzzle for now!

Mini-stars with maxi-mass

When a star explodes and collapses, it becomes incredibly smaller than you might ever expect. It's like breaking up Ping-Pong balls and packing their pieces. Some stars collapse into white dwarf stars. White dwarfs can be smaller than Earth, but they can hold the same amount of matter as the Sun! Even smaller stars, called neutron stars, are formed when very large stars collapse. Neutron stars can be as massive as our Sun, but they might be only a few kilometres in diameter!

The Sun as a Soccer Ball

What if the Sun was...	Then Earth (our home planet) could be...	And Jupiter (the Solar system's biggest planet) would be...	And Pluto (our Solar system's tiniest known planet) could be...	And Alpha Centauri (the nearest star in our Galaxy) would be...
...a soccer ball about 8 3/4 inches (22 cm) wide?	...a pebble less than 1/10 inch (1/4 cm) wide, and about 78 1/2 feet (24 m) from our soccer-ball Sun.	...a bit bigger than a ball bearing 7/8 inch (2.2 cm) wide.	...a pebble tinier even than Earth, and over 1/2 mile (0.8 km) from our soccer-ball Sun.	...nearly 4 miles (6.4 km) from the soccer-ball Sun at the centre of our Solar system.

The Solar System in a Cup

And what if our Solar system was...	Then the Milky Way (our Galaxy) would be...
...small enough to fit in a coffee cup?	...as wide as North America — about 3,000 miles (4,800 km) across!

The Milky Way as a Long-playing Record!

And what if the Milky Way (our Galaxy) was...	Then the Andromeda Galaxy (the galaxy 'next door') would be...	And the farthest-known quasars would be...
...a long-playing record about 1 foot (30 cm) wide?	...23 feet (7 m) away from the Milky Way.	...more than 32 miles (51 km) away from the Milky Way!

As big as we think Earth is, it is only a tiny speck in our vast Universe!

More Books About the Universe

Here are more books that contain information about the Universe. If you are interested in them, look for them in your library or bookshop.

Comets and Meteors. Couper (Franklin Watts)
Discovering Astronomy. Mitton and Mitton (Longman)
Discovering the Sky. de Bergh and Verdet (Hart-Davis)
How Far Away Are the Stars? Gavassi (Cambridge)
Night Sky. Barrett (Franklin Watts)
Our Milky Way and Other Galaxies. Asimov (Gareth Stevens)
Planets. Barrett (Franklin Watts)
The Planets. Couper (Franklin Watts)
The Planets. Jay (Franklin Watts)
Quasars, Pulsars, and Black Holes. Asimov (Gareth Stevens)
The Stars. Couper (Franklin Watts)
The Sun. Couper (Franklin Watts)
The Young Astronomer's Handbook. Ridpath (Hamlyn)

Places to Visit

You can explore many places in the Universe without leaving Earth. Here are some places to visit.

Jodrell Bank Visitors' Centre
Macclesfield, Cheshire

Science Museum
S. Kensington, London

London Planetarium
Marylebone Road, London

Royal Greenwich Observatory
Herstmonceux Castle
Hailsham, E. Sussex

Royal Observatory
Edinburgh, Scotland

There are also planetaria at museums in Southend, Liverpool, National Maritime Museum (Greenwich), Armagh Observatory (N. Ireland), and Mills Observatory, Dundee (Scotland).

For More Information About the Universe

Here are some places you can write to for more information about the Universe. Be sure to tell them exactly what you want to know about or see. Remember to include your age, full name, and address.

For information about astronomy:
NASA Kennedy Space Center
Educational Services Office
Kennedy Space Center, Florida 32899, USA

For photographs of stars and galaxies:
Caltech Bookstore
California Institute of Technology
Mail Code 1-51
Pasadena, California 91125, USA

Glossary

Andromeda Galaxy: the closest spiral galaxy to our own, although it is over 2,000,000 light-years away.

atoms: the smallest particles of elements that can exist. They are the source of nuclear energy when joined together or split apart.

the Big Bang: a gigantic explosion that some scientists believe created our Universe.

billion: in this book, a billion means 1 followed by nine zeroes — 1,000,000,000 (a thousand million). A trillion means 1 followed by 12 zeroes — 1,000,000,000,000 (a million million). These are standard figures in the US and are becoming increasingly common in Britain, too. However, some other British books use the word billion to mean a million million. It is important to check which system a book is using.

black hole: an object in space caused by the explosion and collapse of a star. This object is so tightly packed that not even light can escape the force of its gravity.

Copernicus, Nicolaus: the first modern scholar to suggest, in 1543, that the Sun was at the centre of the Universe, with the planets orbiting around it.

Doppler, Christian: the Austrian scientist who, in 1842, showed why noise sounds more shrill when coming toward you, but sounds deeper when moving away from you. Light waves act in a similar way. They are shorter — and appear blue — when they are coming toward you, and become longer — and appear red — when moving away. (See also **red shift**.)

galaxy: any of the billions of large groupings of stars, gas, and dust that exist in the Universe. Our Galaxy is known as the Milky Way Galaxy.

Herschel, William: the German astronomer who, in 1785, showed that the visible stars are all part of a vast collection of stars. He said that our Sun was part of this collection, which today we know as the Milky Way Galaxy.

light-year: the distance that light travels in one year — nearly 9.6 trillion km.

nebula: a cloud of dust and gas in space. Some large nebulae are the birthplaces of stars. Other nebulae are the debris of dying stars.

neutron stars: very small stars formed when large stars collapse, but which keep much of their very great mass.

optical illusion: something perceived by the eye, a camera, or a telescope that is not what it appears to be. For example, the appearance of a 'bridge' of gases from a quasar to a galaxy may be false, a trick played on the 'eye' of the telescope — an optical illusion.

quasars: the most distant galaxies in the Universe. They are billions of light-years away from Earth.

radio waves: electromagnetic waves that can be detected by radio receiving equipment.

red shift: the apparent reddening of light given off by an object moving away from us (see **Doppler**). The greater the red shift of light from a distant galaxy, the farther that galaxy is moving away from us.

sphere: a globelike body. The ancient Greeks believed that Earth was a large sphere at the centre of the Universe.

supernova: the result of a huge star exploding. When a supernova occurs, material from the star is spread through space.

Universe: everything that we know exists and believe may exist.

variable stars: stars whose brightness changes. Some variable stars change brightness very regularly. Others are unpredictable.

Index

The publishers wish to thank the following for permission to reproduce copyright material: front cover, pp. 17, 19 (both), © Julian Baum, 1988; p. 4 (upper), © Sally Bensusen, 1988; pp. 4 (lower), 8 (upper), 10 (upper), photographs courtesy of Julian Baum; p. 5, © Frank Zullo, 1987; p. 6 (upper), AIP Niels Bohr Library; p. 6 (lower), Mary Evans Picture Library; p. 7, © Anglo-Australian Telescope Board, David Malin, 1980; p. 8 (lower), © George East, 1978; pp. 9, 13, 16, 24 (upper), 25 (lower), National Optical Astronomy Observatories; pp. 10-11, 14-15, © Brian Sullivan, 1988; p. 12, Science Photo Library; pp. 20-21, 22-23, © Paternostro / Schaller, 1988; p. 24 (lower), Jet Propulsion Laboratory; pp. 25 (upper), 26-27, © Mark Paternostro, 1988; pp. 28-29, © Larry Ortiz, 1988.